THE SIXTH FLOOR MUSEUM AT DEALEY PLAZA

411 Elm Street | Dallas, TX 75202 | 214.747.6660

All quotes used in this book are from the Oral History Collection at The Sixth Floor Museum at Dealey Plaza unless otherwise noted.

The Donning Company Publishers
184 Business Park Drive, Suite 206 Virginia Beach, VA 23462

Library of Congress Cataloging-in-Publication Data

The Sixth Floor Museum at Dealey Plaza, Dallas, Texas.

   pages cm
  ISBN 978-1-57864-837-5
1. Kennedy, John F. (John Fitzgerald), 1917-1963--Assassination. 2.
Sixth Floor Museum at Dealey Plaza. I. Sixth Floor Museum at Dealey Plaza.
   E842.9.S525 2013
   973.922092--dc23
                        2013017825

Printed in the United States of America at Walsworth Publishing Company

TABLE OF CONTENTS

FOREWORD

The Sixth Floor Museum at Dealey Plaza is an unparalleled cultural institution that interprets the historical and ongoing narrative of the assassination of President John F. Kennedy. Located within the Dealey Plaza National Historic Landmark District, the Museum offers critical insight and a tangible link to one of the most important events in U.S. history.

Known simply as The Sixth Floor when it opened in 1989, the Museum receives over 350,000 visitors annually. Never could we have imagined that all these years later, audiences from around the world would still be coming to this historic site in Dallas, Texas. Nor could we have imagined that what was initially conceived as a temporary display on the sixth floor of the former Texas School Book Depository would morph into a full-fledged museum with an ever-growing historical collection of documents, photographs, oral histories, films and artifacts.

More than just a destination, visitors come here to experience an unbiased and genuine look into the life, death and legacy of a president and glean more about the lives and emotions of people—past and present—whose stories have captivated the world. As a museum, we are dedicated to collecting stories that have not yet been told and preserving those that have.

Today The Sixth Floor Museum is shifting from capturing and sharing the living memories of "rememberers"—those who lived through the assassination—to an inevitable dependence on this historical record and increasingly distant voices from the past. The Museum's continuing role is to present these voices, stories and historical materials in engaging and inspiring ways for future generations and to document the commemorative programming and interpretation that accompanies each significant milestone.

The assassination of President John F. Kennedy and the events in its aftermath have left an indelible imprint on our country, our collective identity and the national consciousness. It is our shared history that we are honored to have in our care.

Nicola Longford

Nicola Longford
Executive Director
The Sixth Floor Museum at Dealey Plaza

INTRODUCTION

On November 22, 1963, Dallas, Texas, became the focus of world shock, grief and outrage when President John F. Kennedy was assassinated in Dealey Plaza. Investigators found evidence that shots were fired from the sixth floor of the Texas School Book Depository, a school textbook warehouse facing the plaza. Twenty-six years later, The Sixth Floor Exhibit opened on Presidents Day, February 20, 1989. Today the Museum and its core exhibit, *John F. Kennedy and the Memory of a Nation*, recreate the social and political context of the early 1960s, chronicle the assassination and its aftermath, and recognize Kennedy's lasting impact on American culture.

JOHN F. KENNEDY

Senator John F. Kennedy's 1960 presidential campaign was a platform of new ideas, big changes and an exciting new American future. The public was fascinated by Kennedy's glamour and youth, and his inspiring speeches appealed to many voters.

"We should not let our fears hold us back from pursuing our hopes."

—*Senator John F. Kennedy*
Washington, D.C.
December 11, 1959

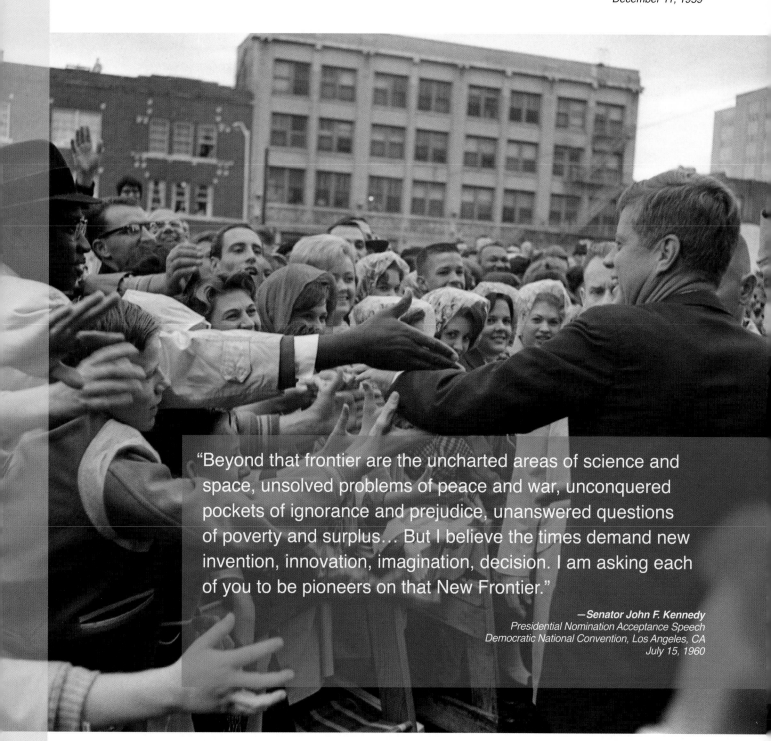

"Beyond that frontier are the uncharted areas of science and space, unsolved problems of peace and war, unconquered pockets of ignorance and prejudice, unanswered questions of poverty and surplus… But I believe the times demand new invention, innovation, imagination, decision. I am asking each of you to be pioneers on that New Frontier."

—*Senator John F. Kennedy*
Presidential Nomination Acceptance Speech
Democratic National Convention, Los Angeles, CA
July 15, 1960

KENNEDY WILL WIN

KENNEDY JOHNSON

LEADERSHIP FOR THE 60's

"As we enter the new decade of the Sixties, America faces challenges greater than any which it has faced before.... This is a time for boldness and energy. This is a time for stout-hearted men who can turn dreams into reality."

—*Senator John F. Kennedy*
Remarks via telephone to
New York State AFLO-CIO
August 30, 1960

"Today we still welcome those winds of change, and we have every reason to believe that our tide is running strong."

—*President John F. Kennedy*
State of the Union Address
January 14, 1963

Campaign ephemera from the Museum's collection.

10

"Let the word go forth from this time and place, to friend and foe alike, that the torch has been passed to a new generation of Americans.

And so, my fellow Americans, ask not what your country can do for you—ask what you can do for your country. My fellow citizens of the world: ask not what America will do for you, but what together we can do for the freedom of man."

—President John F. Kennedy
Inaugural Address
Washington, D.C.
January 20, 1961

PRESIDENT KENNEDY'S TRIP TO TEXAS

By the fall of 1963, President Kennedy was looking ahead to his 1964 re-election campaign. There was a political rift among Texas Democrats—and Texas was a key state for the election. The President planned a quick trip to San Antonio, Houston, Fort Worth, Dallas and Austin in an effort to mend fences and reinvigorate his Texan supporters.

Jacqueline Kennedy accompanied her husband to Texas, her first public tour since the death of the Kennedys' infant son Patrick on August 9, 1963. Vice President Lyndon B. Johnson was joined by Lady Bird Johnson. Texas Governor John Connally and his wife Nellie served as hosts for the presidential party at each stop.

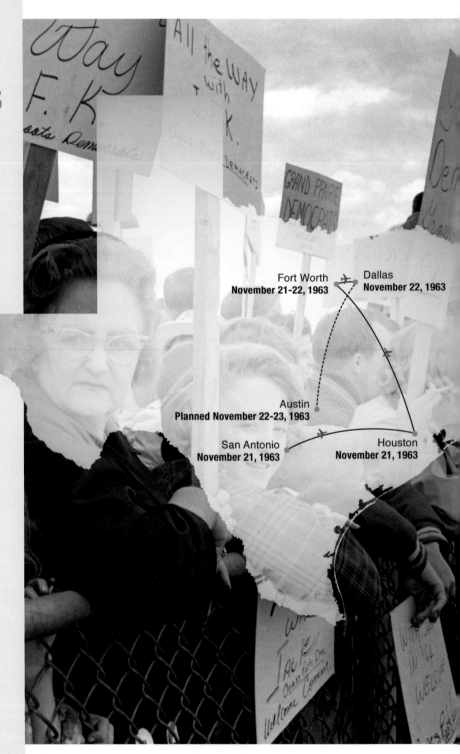

Fort Worth
November 21-22, 1963

Dallas
November 22, 1963

Austin
Planned November 22-23, 1963

San Antonio
November 21, 1963

Houston
November 21, 1963

"It was Presidential politics pure and simple. It was the opening effort of the 1964 campaign. And it was going beautifully."

—*Lyndon B. Johnson*
The Vantage Point: Perspectives of the Presidency, 1963-1969
Published in 1971

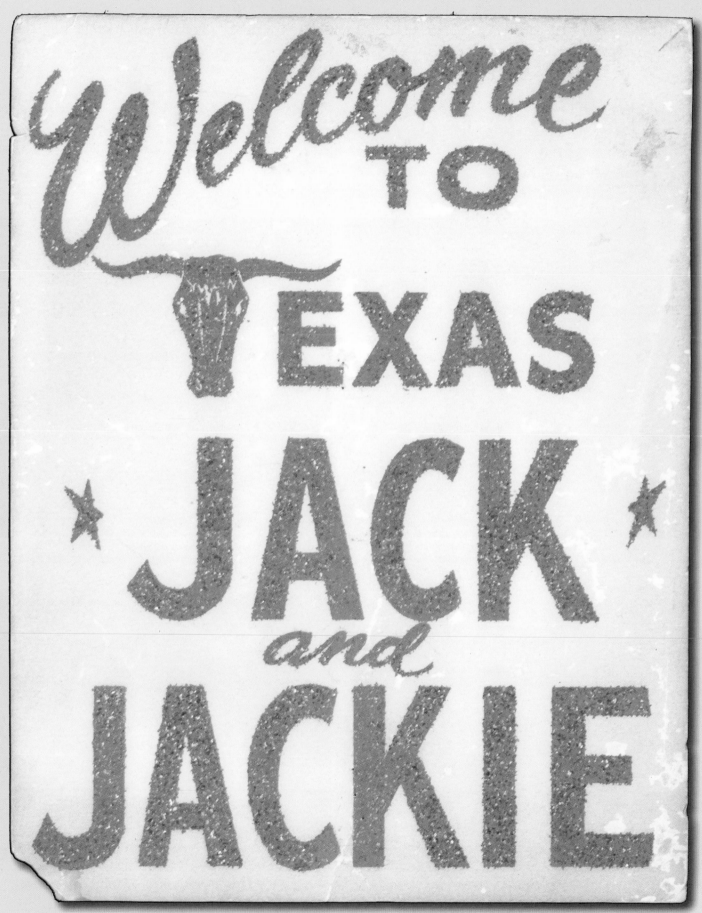

Welcome TO TEXAS JACK and JACKIE

Locally-produced sign used to welcome the Kennedys at Carswell Air Force Base in Fort Worth on November 21, 1963.

The first day of the trip was a huge success. Large, enthusiastic crowds greeted President Kennedy and his wife in San Antonio, Houston and Fort Worth, the first three cities of the tour. The second day began with light rain in Fort Worth, but the weather had cleared by the time the President's party left for Dallas. It appeared the Kennedys would experience the same success and warm welcome they had seen the day before.

President and Mrs. Kennedy arriving to dedicate a new aerospace medical center in San Antonio on November 21, 1963.

First Lady Jacqueline Kennedy addressing the League of United Latin American Citizens in Spanish at a dinner in Houston the evening of November 21, 1963.

President Kennedy, followed by Texas Governor John Connally, walking from the Hotel Texas to the parking lot to address the crowd of supporters that gathered there in the rain the morning of November 22, 1963.

President and Mrs. Kennedy greeting the crowd at Dallas Love Field Airport on Friday, November 22, 1963.

-2-

Press badge worn by Vivian Castleberry, women's editor of the Dallas Times Herald newspaper. She was assigned to cover the luncheon at the Dallas Trade Mart scheduled to take place after the Dallas motorcade that Friday.

The Dallas Trade Mart luncheon and the Texas Welcome Dinner in Austin never took place.

PRESIDENT KENNEDY'S VISIT TO DALLAS NOVEMBER 22, 1963

PRESS

Invitation to the Dallas Trade Mart luncheon.

Place setting at the Dallas Trade Mart luncheon intended for President Kennedy; currently on loan to The Sixth Floor Museum.

The Dallas Citizens Council
The Dallas Assembly
The Science Research Center
request the pleasure of
the company of

Mr. & Mrs. Lee M. Ferby

at a luncheon in honor of
The President and Mrs. Kennedy
The Vice-President and Mrs. Johnson
The Governor and Mrs. Connally
Friday, the twenty-second of November
at twelve noon
The Trade Mart

Gold paper ticket to attend the Texas Welcome Dinner, planned to welcome the Kennedys and the Johnsons to Austin the evening of the 22nd.

THE STATE DEMOCRATIC EXECUTIVE COMMITTEE

TEXAS WELCOME DINNER

IN HONOR OF

PRESIDENT JOHN F. KENNEDY

AND

VICE PRESIDENT LYNDON B. JOHNSON

MUNICIPAL AUDITORIUM   CITY OF AUSTIN

SEVEN-THIRTY O'CLOCK
FRIDAY EVENING
NOVEMBER 22, 1963   № D15201

ADMIT ONE   ★   OPTIONAL DRESS

Texas Welcome

Texas welcomes the President
of the United States
and the Vice President
of the United States

Program to the Texas Welcome Dinner in Austin.

15

Friday, November 22, 1963

8:45 a.m. President John F. Kennedy speaks to supporters in the parking lot of the Hotel Texas in Fort Worth.

9:00 – 11:00 a.m. The Kennedys attend a formal breakfast at the Hotel Texas, then head to Carswell Air Force Base to board Air Force One for Dallas.

11:40 a.m. Air Force One arrives at Love Field. After greeting the crowd, President Kennedy's motorcade heads toward downtown.

12.30 p.m. President Kennedy and Texas Governor John Connally shot in Dealey Plaza in Dallas.

12:35 p.m. President Kennedy arrives at Parkland Hospital.

12:45 p.m. Police broadcast first description of a suspect: *The suspect from Elm and Houston is reported to be an unknown white male about 30, slender build, 5 feet 10 inches tall, 165 pounds, armed with what is thought to be a 30-30 rifle.*

1:00 p.m. Parkland doctors pronounce Kennedy dead.

1:12 p.m. Police find three empty rifle shells near the southeast-corner window of the sixth floor of the Book Depository.

1:15 p.m. Police officer J.D. Tippit shot and killed in the Oak Cliff neighborhood of Dallas.

1:22 p.m. Dallas police officers find a rifle hidden in the northwest corner of the Depository's sixth floor.

1:30 p.m. At Parkland, Assistant White House Press Secretary Malcolm Kilduff officially announces President Kennedy's death.

1:50 p.m. Lee Harvey Oswald arrested at the Texas Theatre in Oak Cliff.

2:08 p.m. Hearse with President Kennedy's body and Jacqueline Kennedy leaves Parkland Hospital for Dallas Love Field Airport.

2:20 p.m. Interrogation of suspect Lee Harvey Oswald begins at Dallas police headquarters.

2:38 p.m. Lyndon B. Johnson takes the oath of office aboard Air Force One.

5:10 p.m. President Johnson makes his first statement to the nation from Andrews Air Force Base in Maryland.

7:00 p.m. Kennedy autopsy begins at Bethesda Naval Hospital.

7:10 p.m. Oswald charged with the murder of Officer Tippit.

Saturday, November 23, 1963

12:00 a.m. Midnight press showing with Lee Harvey Oswald held in basement of Dallas Police headquarters. Local nightclub owner Jack Ruby attends.

1:30 a.m. Oswald charged with the murder of President Kennedy.

2:10 a.m. Oswald fingerprinted and photographed by police.

4:00 a.m. Oswald identified as the owner of the rifle found at the Depository.

9:00 a.m. In D.C., private mass held for Kennedy family and friends in the White House East Room.

1:30 p.m. President Johnson holds first Cabinet meeting.
...John Fitzgerald Kennedy, 35th President of the United States, has been taken from us by an act which outrages decent men everywhere... As he did not shrink from his responsibilities, but welcomed them, so he would not have us shrink from carrying on his work beyond this hour of national tragedy... therefore, I, Lyndon B. Johnson...do appoint Monday next, November 25...a national day of mourning.

Sunday, November 24, 1963

11:21 a.m. During a transfer of prisoner Lee Harvey Oswald from city jail to county jail, Jack Ruby shoots Oswald. Ruby is immediately taken into custody.

12:08 p.m. President Kennedy's casket leaves the White House in procession to the U.S. Capitol for memorial services.

1:07 p.m. Oswald dies of gunshot wound at Parkland Hospital.

3:15 p.m. Jack Ruby is escorted to the office of Dallas Police Captain J.W. "Will" Fritz for formal questioning and arraignment on a charge of murder.

Monday, November 25, 1963

1:00 a.m. Line of mourners outside Capitol Rotunda is three miles long.

10:30 a.m. – 12:30 p.m. President Kennedy's funeral. Caisson leaves White House for funeral at St. Matthew's Cathedral. Mrs. Kennedy, family and 100 world leaders follow on foot. After the service, John F. Kennedy, Jr., salutes his father's casket. It is his third birthday.

2:13 p.m. Kennedy's widow and brother light eternal flame at grave site in Arlington National Cemetery.

3:15 p.m. Officer Tippit buried in Dallas; funeral attended by 700 officers.

4:15 p.m. Oswald buried in Fort Worth; reporters serve as pallbearers.

All times Central Standard Time (CST)

RECEPTION IN DALLAS

Dallas was the most conservative city on the President's Texas itinerary. With a metropolitan population of one million, the city was the financial and business center of the state. Small but vocal extremist groups in Dallas had made national headlines the month before the President's visit when United Nations Ambassador Adlai Stevenson was spat upon and hit on the head with a placard. That incident and others caused some of the President's advisors to have serious concerns over his trip to Dallas, and extra security measures were put into place.

Although some propagandists distributed anti-Kennedy flyers and ran a highly critical advertisement in the local newspaper in advance of the Kennedys' visit, the presidential party was welcomed by large and enthusiastic crowds in Dallas, with some estimates running as high as 250,000 people—a quarter of the city's population.

WANTED

FOR

TREASON

THIS MAN is wanted for treasonous activities against the United States:

1. Betraying the Constitution (which he swore to uphold):
He is turning the sovereignty of the U. S. over to the communist controlled United Nations.
He is betraying our friends (Cuba, Katanga, Portugal) and befriending our enemies (Russia, Yugoslavia, Poland).

2. He has been WRONG on innumerable issues affecting the security of the U.S. (United Nations-Berlin wall-Missle removal-Cuba-Wheat deals-Test Ban Treaty, etc.)

3. He has been lax in enforcing Communist Registration laws.

4. He has given support and encouragement to the Communist inspired racial riots.

5. He has illegally invaded a sovereign State with federal troops.

6. He has consistently appointed Anti-Christians to Federal office: Upholds the Supreme Court in its Anti-Christian rulings. Aliens and known Communists abound in Federal offices.

7. He has been caught in fantastic LIES to the American people (including personal ones like his previous marrage and divorce).

Copies of this flyer were distributed by anti-Kennedy propagandists in Dallas in the days preceding President Kennedy's visit to Dallas, placed on car windshields and tucked inside the racks of the two Dallas daily newspapers.

"There's Mrs. Kennedy and the crowd yells, and the president of the United States. And I can see his suntan all the way from here. Shaking hands now with the Dallas people, Governor and Mrs. Connally."

—*Bob Walker*
News Director, WFAA-TV/Dallas
November 22, 1963

DALLAS
LOVE FIELD
AIRPORT

Denton Dr.

Mockingbird Ln.

MOTORCADE ROUTE
November 22, 1963

11:40 a.m.

Lemmon Ave.

Central Expressway

Harry Hines Blvd.

PARKLAND
MEMORIAL
HOSPITAL

12:35 p.m.

Stemmons Frwy.

DALLAS
TRADE MART

Harry Hines Blvd.

Turtle Creek Blvd.

Cedar Springs Blvd.

Stemmons Frwy.

Harwood St.

TEXAS
SCHOOL BOOK
DEPOSITORY

Elm St.
Main St.
Commerce St.

N

Commerce St.

DEALEY
PLAZA

Houston St.

"The streets were lined with people—lots and lots of people—the children all smiling; placards, confetti; people waving from windows."

—*Lady Bird Johnson*
A White House Diary
2007

These images show the presidential motorcade at various points along its route through Dallas.

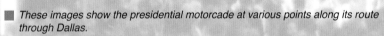

"Here comes the first car with Police Chief Jesse Curry and Sheriff Bill Decker, and here is the President of the United States. And what a crowd—what a tremendous welcome he is getting now. And there's Jackie. She's getting just as big a welcome. And the crowd is absolutely going wild. This is a friendly crowd in downtown Dallas as the President and First Lady pass by…"

—Bob Huffaker
KRLD Radio
November 22, 1963

"Mr. President, you can't say Dallas doesn't love you."

—Nellie Connally
As the presidential limousine turned onto Houston Street, 12:29 p.m.
From Love Field: Our Final Hours with President John F. Kennedy
2003

"Let's get out of here; we are hit."

—*Secret Service Agent Roy Kellerman*
From the presidential limousine, 12:30 p.m.
Warren Commission Report, Vol. 2
1964

SHOTS IN DEALEY PLAZA

As the motorcade neared the end of the parade route, the President's party was looking ahead to the next stop—a bipartisan lunch with 2,600 guests at the Dallas Trade Mart. But at 12:30 p.m. shots rang out in Dealey Plaza.

The images and the quotes on these pages are from eyewitnesses to the Kennedy assassination, drawn from the Museum's collection of photographs, home movies and oral histories.

"...and I heard 'bang, bang.'"

—Marilyn Sitzman

"The last shot that we heard was right in front of us and it was like the same sound— far off and to the left— but I saw his head open up. So, of course, by this time I knew it wasn't firecrackers."

—Marilyn Sitzman

"I can remember hearing a Boom! Boom!"

—Bill Newman

"I saw the president grab at his throat and lurch to his left, so I knew something was wrong, something had happened."

—Clint Hill

"And just as the president got straight in front of us... the third shot rang out. And I can remember seeing the side of President Kennedy's head come off. ... and she hollered out, 'Oh my God, no! They've shot Jack!'"

—Bill Newman

"...I was wondering what kind of idiot would be throwing firecrackers as the president drove by."

—James Tague

"So I jumped from the car and ran toward the presidential vehicle."

—Clint Hill

"...Turned back to the car and heard two more shots and saw him fall."

—Ann Atterberry

"All I could think was, 'They killed him. They killed him.' That's all I could think."

—Marilyn Sitzman

Dallas dress manufacturer Abraham Zapruder filmed the Kennedy assassination with an 8mm Bell & Howell home movie camera. Although it remains open to interpretation, his film shows the President during the entire assassination and is the most complete visual record of events in Dealey Plaza that day.

The Sixth Floor Museum displays many of the cameras used by amateur photographers and filmmakers who witnessed the assassination. The original home movie camera used by Abraham Zapruder, pictured left, is held at the National Archives.

 The president's limousine racing from Dealey Plaza to Parkland Memorial Hospital.

DEALEY PLAZA TO WASHINGTON, D.C.

President Kennedy had been shot. The lead cars raced up Stemmons Freeway, past the Trade Mart, taking the President to Parkland Memorial Hospital. Crowds gathered outside Parkland as rumors of the shooting spread. Listening to car radios, people waited anxiously for news. At 1:30 p.m. Assistant White House Press Secretary Malcolm Kilduff held a press conference at Parkland to announce that President Kennedy was dead. The news spread around the world with astonishing speed. Lyndon B. Johnson, now president of the United States, left the hospital, followed by Jacqueline Kennedy escorting her husband's casket.

"There was no screaming in that horrible car. It was just a silent, terrible drive."

—*Nellie Connally*
U.S. House Select Committee on Assassinations Report
1978

Guests at the Dallas Trade Mart luncheon praying for the president after hearing of the shooting.

Crowds gathered outside Parkland Memorial Hospital, awaiting news of the president's condition.

"…a priest walked out, he said, 'At one p.m. the president died.' And I couldn't believe it. It was like God, no, please no, no, no, no, no. That's all I can remember."

—*Kathey Atkinson*
Parkland Hospital bystander
2011

"President John F. Kennedy died at approximately one o'clock, Central Standard Time today here in Dallas. He died of a gunshot wound in the brain."

—*Malcolm Kilduff*
Assistant White House
Press Secretary
Press conference at
Parkland Memorial Hospital
1:30 p.m., November 22, 1963

The white hearse outside Parkland used to transport the president's casket to Air Force One at Dallas Love Field for the flight back to Washington, D.C.

Once on Air Force One back at Dallas Love Field, President Lyndon B. Johnson was officially sworn in by Judge Sarah T. Hughes, and the plane left for Washington, D.C.

"I do solemnly swear that I will faithfully execute the office of President of the United States, and will to the best of my ability, preserve, protect, and defend the Constitution of the United States. So help me God."

—*Lyndon Baines Johnson*
November 22, 1963,
2:38 p.m.

TEXAS SCHOOL BOOK DEPOSITORY

Within minutes of the shooting in Dealey Plaza, police began searching the Texas School Book Depository, a school textbook warehouse at the corners of Elm and Houston streets. Witnesses reported seeing a rifle in one of its windows and others said they had heard shots coming from the building. Investigators found three spent bullet shells beneath an open window in the southeast corner of the Depository's sixth floor. Shortly after, police discovered a Mannlicher-Carcano rifle hidden between boxes stacked in the northwest corner on the same floor.

"That's when I found the… [boxes of] books had been stacked and a crease in 'em where the rifle laid appeared to be. Of course, the rifle wasn't there, but you could see the crease… And down here, besides where the rifle was when he ejected the shells, there were three spent shells…

I hollered, 'Mr. Decker,' I says, 'Tell Mr. Fritz to send his crime lab up here. I've got something.' And that's all I told him."

—Luke Mooney
Dallas County Deputy Sheriff
2002

■ *Deputy Sheriff Luke Mooney's badge.*

This enameled metal sign hung over the southeast corner entrance to the Texas School Book Depository in 1963. Today it is on display at The Sixth Floor Museum.

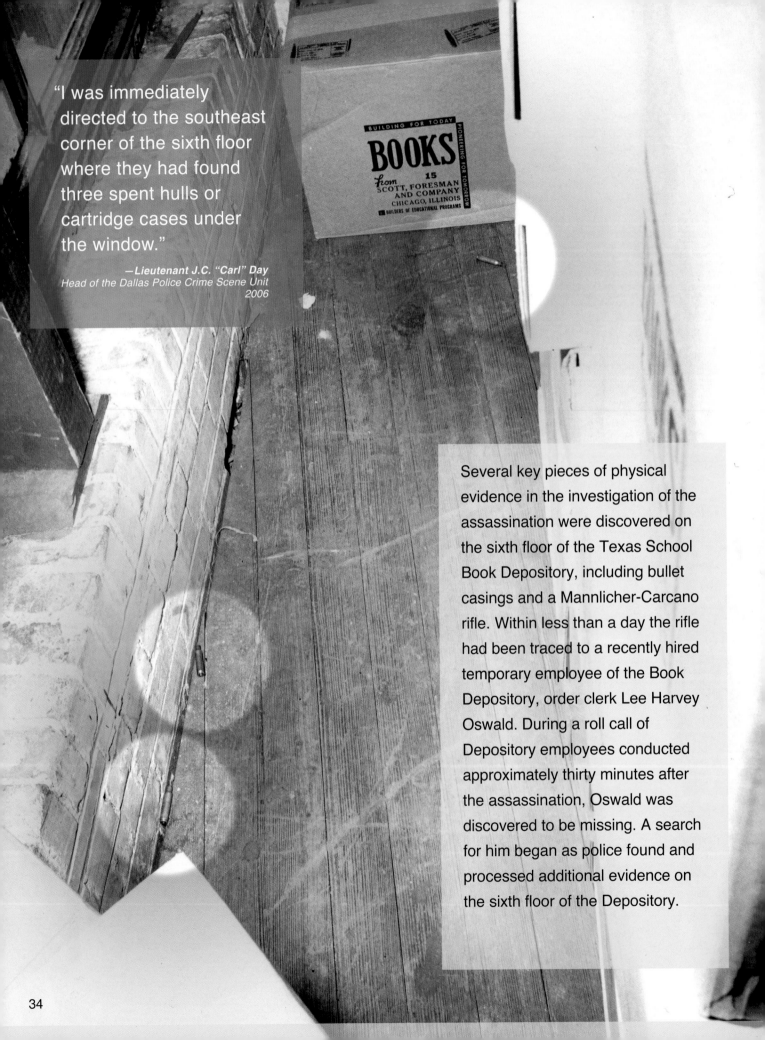

"I was immediately directed to the southeast corner of the sixth floor where they had found three spent hulls or cartridge cases under the window."

—*Lieutenant J.C. "Carl" Day*
Head of the Dallas Police Crime Scene Unit
2006

BUILDING FOR TODAY
PIONEERING FOR TOMORROW

BOOKS
15
from
SCOTT, FORESMAN
AND COMPANY
CHICAGO, ILLINOIS
BUILDERS OF EDUCATIONAL PROGRAMS

Several key pieces of physical evidence in the investigation of the assassination were discovered on the sixth floor of the Texas School Book Depository, including bullet casings and a Mannlicher-Carcano rifle. Within less than a day the rifle had been traced to a recently hired temporary employee of the Book Depository, order clerk Lee Harvey Oswald. During a roll call of Depository employees conducted approximately thirty minutes after the assassination, Oswald was discovered to be missing. A search for him began as police found and processed additional evidence on the sixth floor of the Depository.

Boxes were stacked around the southeast corner window on the sixth floor.

Dallas police officer Jerry Hill leans out a Depository window to talk with colleagues on the ground outside the building. Several police officers and journalists used this direct method of communication throughout investigations that day.

"The search seemed to center on the School Book Depository at that time… Officer Luke Mooney, a deputy, found what's later been referred to as the 'sniper's nest' over in the window area, and like most police officers, we had to go over and take a look at it and see what it looked like.

… There were boxes set up to create what appeared to be a rifle rest for somebody shooting out the window. There were some spent shells right here on the floor, and there was also a brown bag with some partially eaten lunch. And it was just kind of a unsettling feeling came across me."

—Eugene Boone
Dallas County Deputy Sheriff
2003

View from the window allegedly used by the presidential assassin.

"And so, I found the rifle. [I] said, 'Here's the rifle,' and tried to protect the scene from any officers. Officers are bad about tearing up a crime scene—contaminating, I should say, a crime scene. And tried to protect that. Lieutenant J.C. Day with the Dallas Police Department came and photographed and removed the weapon, and then I think later gave it to Captain Will Fritz."

—Eugene Boone
Dallas County Deputy Sheriff
2003

The rifle was taken to the Dallas Police Department and examined for fingerprints and other evidence. Investigations conducted by the head of the Crime Scene Unit, Lieutenant J.C. "Carl" Day, were cut short. The Federal Bureau of Investigation collected the rifle and all related evidence from Day at 11:45 p.m. on November 22, 1963.

Lieutenant J.C. "Carl" Day, indicating the location in the northwest corner of the sixth floor of the Book Depository where a Mannlicher-Carcano rifle was found.

The rifle in its hiding place.

Fingerprints on the rifle.

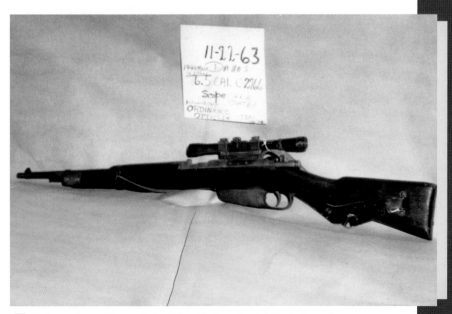

Dallas police evidence photo of the rifle found at the Book Depository.

"I was working at the southeast corner window when they found the rifle in the northwest corner… We went over there where it was. As far as I know I was the first one to get a hold of it. From its position here, I picked it up in such a way that I wouldn't destroy any fingerprints that might be on it. The rifle had a weather-beaten strap on it, and it was apparent that you could not get a fingerprint off that old, rough strap…I told Captain Fritz that this warehouse was not the place to try to work on this gun. So I took it back to the City Hall and locked it up in an evidence box."

—Lieutenant J.C. "Carl" Day
Head of the Dallas Police Crime Scene Unit
2006

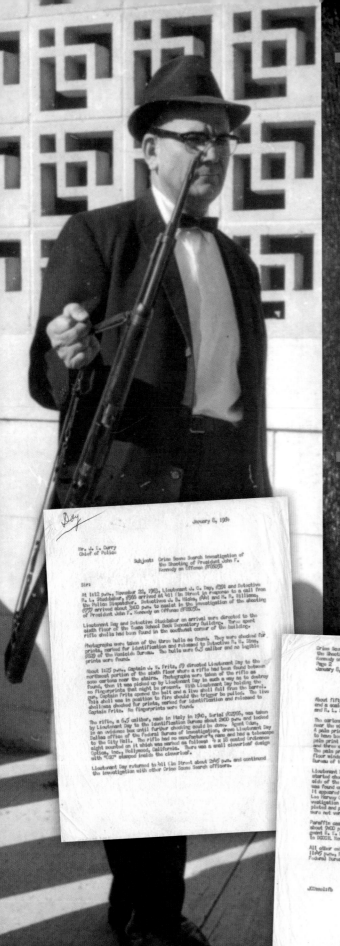

Lieutenant Day carrying the rifle out of the Book Depository.

The fingerprint powder and the brush used by Lieutenant Day to process the rifle for fingerprints.

FINGER PRINT POWDER

Manufactured by
CRIMINAL RESEARCH PRODUCTS, INC
CONSHOHOCKEN, PENNSYLVANIA

"The fingerprints were found on the side of the rifle near the trigger and magazine housing and a palm print was found on the underside of the gun barrel on the end of the stock. It appeared probable these prints were from the right palm and fingers of Lee Harvey Oswald..."

—*Memo from Lieutenant Carl Day to Mr. J.E. Curry, Chief of Police*
January 8, 1964

Typewritten memo in the Museum's collection by Lieutenant Day explaining how he examined the rifle for evidence on November 22, 1963.

"Oswald was the type of individual that wanted to be somebody important... He didn't shoot John F. Kennedy. He shot the president of the United States because that would get him notoriety and recognition."

—*Jim Leavelle*
Dallas Police Detective who interrogated Oswald
2002

A SUSPECT ARRESTED

In Dallas's Oak Cliff neighborhood, Police Officer J.D. Tippit stopped a man who fit the general description of the shooting suspect. In front of eyewitnesses the man shot Tippit four times with a .38 revolver. The same man was then seen entering the nearby Texas Theatre. After a struggle during which the suspect attempted to shoot the arresting officer at point-blank range, police were able to apprehend the suspect. He was found to be the missing Depository employee, Lee Harvey Oswald. He was arrested and taken to Dallas Police headquarters less than ninety minutes after President Kennedy was shot in Dealey Plaza.

While Oswald was being interrogated, hundreds of members of the world press descended on the police station. They crowded the halls, hoping for a glimpse of the suspect and more information about the alleged assassin.

The Texas Theatre in Oak Cliff, where Oswald was arrested. During the scuffle he attempted to shoot the arresting officer.

Officers and reporters observe a moment of silence for J.D. Tippit.

39

Police searched residences in Oak Cliff and Irving that were associated with Oswald. An ex-Marine who had defected to the Soviet Union, Oswald and his Russian-born wife Marina lived intermittently in the Dallas/Fort Worth area during 1962–1963. Investigators and the media immediately began to assemble a portrait of the suspect as a disgruntled left-wing loner.

Lee Harvey Oswald, alias Alek J. Hidell or O.H. Lee, was arraigned for Officer Tippit's murder on Friday night, less than seven hours after the assassination of President Kennedy. Six hours after his arraignment for Tippit's murder, Oswald was formally charged with killing President John F. Kennedy.

Lee Harvey Oswald in custody at Dallas Police headquarters, November 22, 1963.

"The scene at the police station was just bedlam. I mean, you couldn't move…there were so many people in the halls."

—*Bob Jackson*
Dallas Times Herald *photographer*
1993

Lee Harvey Oswald photographed in his backyard in March 1963 holding the rifle later connected to the Kennedy assassination.

Oswald at the Dallas Police Department's midnight press showing held late Friday, early Saturday, November 23, 1963.

"I really don't know what the situation is about. Nobody has told me anything except that I am accused of murdering a policeman. I know nothing more than that, and I do request someone to come forward to give me legal assistance."

When asked, "Did you kill the President?" Oswald replied, "No. I have not been charged with that. In fact, nobody has said that to me yet. The first thing I heard about it was when the newspaper reporters in the hall asked me that question."

—*Lee Harvey Oswald*
Responding to questions during the midnight press showing November 22–23, 1963

ANOTHER SHOOTING

During a transfer from the Dallas Police headquarters to the county jail, Lee Harvey Oswald was escorted through the building's basement garage by several Dallas police detectives. The press was there as well. A man in a grey fedora stepped out from the crowd and shot Oswald. The man, local nightclub owner Jack Ruby, was immediately arrested and taken into custody. Oswald died less than two hours later at Parkland Memorial Hospital, never having regained consciousness.

THE DALLAS TIMES HERALD — FINAL EDITION

Mourning Nation Bids Chief Farewell

Tip to FBI Warned of Oswald Death

The President's accused killer as executioner's bullet pierces body.

Anonymous Call Forecast Slaying During Transfer | **Nation Buries Its Chief**

Pulitzer Prize-winning photograph taken by Dallas Times Herald photographer Bob Jackson in the basement of Dallas Police headquarters.

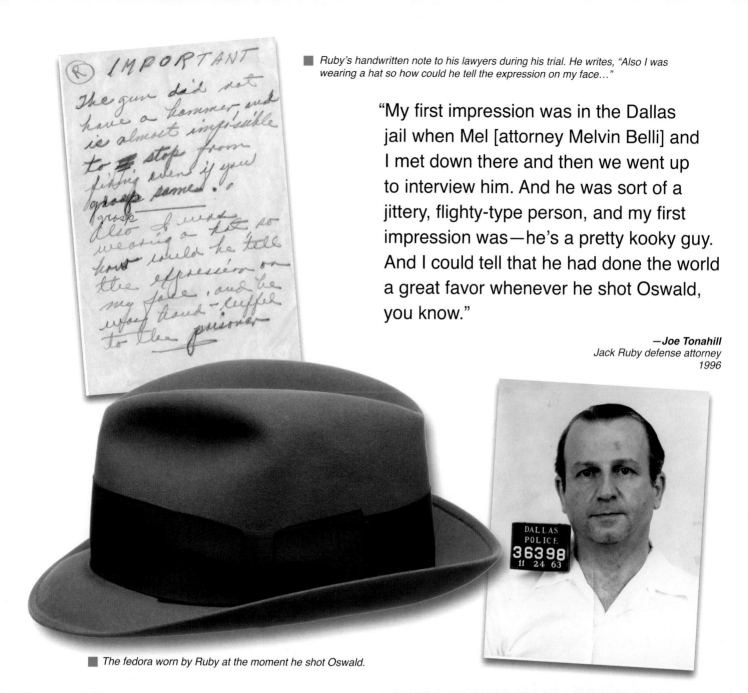

Ruby's handwritten note to his lawyers during his trial. He writes, "Also I was wearing a hat so how could he tell the expression on my face..."

"My first impression was in the Dallas jail when Mel [attorney Melvin Belli] and I met down there and then we went up to interview him. And he was sort of a jittery, flighty-type person, and my first impression was—he's a pretty kooky guy. And I could tell that he had done the world a great favor whenever he shot Oswald, you know."

—Joe Tonahill
Jack Ruby defense attorney
1996

The fedora worn by Ruby at the moment he shot Oswald.

Jack Ruby soon went to trial and was found guilty of murder with malice on March 14, 1964. The verdict was later overturned and a new trial was set to begin in the spring of 1967. However, in December 1966, Ruby became ill and was moved from Dallas County Jail to Parkland Memorial Hospital where he was found to be suffering from cancer. He died of a pulmonary embolism on January 3, 1967.

Images of Jack Ruby and two of his lawyers, Joe Tonahill and Melvin Belli.

Jack Ruby and his lawyer Phil Burleson in Ruby's jail cell.

Jack Ruby murder trial jury, 1964.

"I'd look at Ruby sitting there in that courtroom day after day, and I felt very sorry for him. He looked so alone, and I thought he really looked pitiful…He never smiled. …I was hoping all the time that he'd get up and say something, but he never said a word. He wouldn't try to defend himself."

—*J. Waymon Rose*
Ruby trial juror
2002

MOURNING THE PRESIDENT

Within hours of the shooting, Dallas residents began leaving flowers, notes and other tributes to their fallen president in Dealey Plaza. Businesses closed and most people stayed home to watch the story as it unfolded on their televisions.

"A dark spirit had descended on the community. Amazing rumors began to fly… All of the usual suspects were mentioned as possibly having something to do with it. It was blamed on the Russians. It was blamed on the Cubans. It was a very hard day in Dallas life. Nobody had any real answers to all of the questions that were coming up, and it was a real depressing effect on the entire community."

—*Glen Gatlin*
Motorcade spectator
2003

Upon hearing of President Kennedy's death, Pat Sanders sewed a black border around this flag and the Sanders family hung it on their front door.

"For people like me who had grown up in segregation, to hear that John Kennedy had been killed, as far as I was concerned hope had been assassinated. He was our hope."

—**Bob Ray Sanders**
1963 Fort Worth high school student
2007

"I think they actually closed the school down when the news finally came he was dead. I think they sent us all home because everyone was too upset. And I remember just spending the rest of the afternoon kind of in a fog and disbelief and amazement and sadness. It was very, very sad."

—**Diana Chase**
1963 Dallas high school student
2010

CLOSED
DUE TO THE
PRESIDENT'S DEATH

The Texas Theatre, where suspect Lee Harvey Oswald was arrested, closed due to the assassination.

"...All you could do was stand there, look straight ahead, give no signs of breathing, try not to blink, absolutely motionless... The only thing that was really functioning, unfortunately, was the mind. You just get caught up in the time—or you had to be careful not to get caught up in the emotion of the moment, that right below you was the president of the United States."

—Lieutenant William Lee
Commander of the U.S. Marine Corps Silent Drill Platoon
2007

Lieutenant William Lee at the head of the president's casket in the East Room of the White House.

48

In Washington, D.C., hundreds of thousands of people lined up to view the president as he lay in state in the U.S. Capitol Building for two days. Similar crowds lined the route of the funeral cortege during President Kennedy's funeral on Monday, November 25, 1963. President Johnson declared the day a national day of mourning.

■ A veiled Mrs. Kennedy, accompanied by the president's brothers, walked at the head of the procession to the church for the funeral mass.

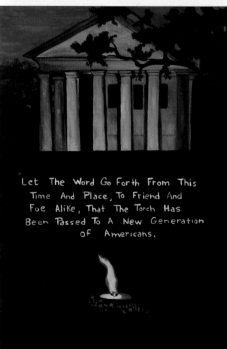

'Let The Word Go Forth From This Time And Place, To Friend And Foe Alike, That The Torch Has Been Passed To A New Generation of Americans.

𝕵𝖔𝖍𝖓 𝕱𝖎𝖙𝖟𝖌𝖊𝖗𝖆𝖑𝖉 𝕶𝖊𝖓𝖓𝖊𝖉𝖞

35th President of the United States
Born May 29, 1917
Inaugurated January 20, 1961
Died November 22, 1963

■ Robert Kennedy and Jacqueline Kennedy kneeling at the president's grave, April 1964.

■ Oil painting by folk artist Bernadine Stetzel.

■ Mass cards for the fallen Catholic president were widely distributed.

49

November 29, 1963
President Lyndon B. Johnson establishes The President's Commission on the Assassination of President Kennedy, led by Supreme Court Chief Justice Earl Warren, to investigate the assassination.

May 23–24, 1964
Members of the Warren Commission and of the FBI spend two days in Dallas recreating the assassination in order to take measurements and analyze evidence.

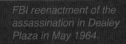

FBI reenactment of the assassination in Dealey Plaza in May 1964.

September 24, 1964
Members of the Warren Commission present copies of their Final Report to President Johnson. Publication of the report is soon followed by the publication of twenty-six volumes of the Commission's hearings and exhibits.

1976
The House of Representatives establishes the House Select Committee on Assassinations to reopen the investigation of the assassination in light of allegations that previous inquiries had not received the full cooperation of federal agencies.

Microphones set up in Dealey Plaza as part of an acoustical study for the House Select Committee on Assassinations, August 20, 1978.

March 29, 1979
The House Select Committee on Assassinations, which also investigated the death of Dr. Martin Luther King Jr., issues its final report.

October 26, 1992
President George H. W. Bush signs the President John F. Kennedy Assassination Records Collection Act into law. One provision of the law mandates that all assassination-related material be housed in a single collection in the National Archives and Records Administration (NARA).

THE INVESTIGATIONS

Almost from the moment of President Kennedy's death, critics have contested the official findings of different investigators. Many aspects of assassination evidence seem contradictory. Conflicting witness testimony about the number and origin of shots, confusion over the location of wounds, discrepancies in medical reporting, and skepticism that a "magic bullet" could have caused wounds to both President Kennedy and Governor Connally led to immediate and continuing controversy about the validity of the Warren Commission's findings and the authenticity of the evidence itself.

The Warren Commission examined approximately 510 visuals during its investigations; the 1976–1978 House Select Committee on Assassinations evaluated these, plus the autopsy photographs, X-rays and some additional photographs of the assassination not previously examined. The House Committee also benefited from independent scientific work that had been done to clarify the Zapruder film. It used new chemical processes and photographic digital enhancement techniques.

Although local investigators built a strong case against Lee Harvey Oswald within days of the shooting, researchers have continued to raise legitimate questions about the assassination in the decades since. Today, a large number of Americans support the idea of a conspiracy. Most agree that this complicated murder mystery will never be fully resolved.

"I never believed that Oswald acted alone, though I can accept that he pulled the trigger."

—*Lyndon B. Johnson*
Atlantic Monthly, *July 1973*

"Why are people so drawn to this conspiracy idea? I think a significant part of it has to do with the fact that people can't accept that someone as inconsequential as Oswald could have killed someone as consequential as Kennedy."

—*Robert Dallek*
Author of An Unfinished Life: John F. Kennedy 1917-1963

"Why are they all lone nuts? Why is there only ever... It's only one person all the time? These people never, ever, you know, talked to anyone else? No one ever helps them?"

—*Jesse Ventura*
Co-author of American Conspiracies

"We have a pristine bullet which according to the Warren Commission is the bullet that passed through Kennedy's neck area, then continued on to strike Connally under the right armpit, to pulverize his fifth rib and blow a hole the size of a silver dollar out of the front of his chest, to continue on to shatter the radius, the large bone in his wrist, and continue on and finally embed itself in his thigh. So we have a bullet which is virtually pristine which is alleged to have done all that, which makes it a very curious bullet indeed."

—*Josiah Thompson*
Author of Six Seconds in Dallas

"That bullet ballistically came from Oswald's rifle, the bullet that passed through President Kennedy's neck did indeed strike the President and Governor Connally. It had to be that one bullet."

—*David Belin*
Warren Commission lawyer

"...I can say absolutely unequivocally that there is nothing that overcomes the conclusion of the Warren Commission that Lee Harvey Oswald was the lone gunman who killed President Kennedy."

—*David Belin*
Warren Commission lawyer

"Clearly the job of the commission was to find that a lone nut, Lee Harvey Oswald, killed the President and that hence the assassination had no more political significance than had the President's plane been struck by lightning."

—*Josiah Thompson*
Author of Six Seconds in Dallas

ONGOING INTEREST IN THE ASSASSINATION

The events of the Kennedy assassination have perplexed, fascinated, saddened and inspired people from the moment the first shots rang out. Hundreds of thousands of people travel to Dealey Plaza and the former Texas School Book Depository every year to visit the site—to feel the pull of history in this place that looks much the same now as it did then. They wonder "what if…?" and speculate on alternative histories. Conspiracy theories abound, and always will, because no one knows for sure exactly what happened here on November 22, 1963.

Dealey Plaza is a National Historic Landmark District dedicated in 1993 on the 30th anniversary of the assassination. The Sixth Floor Museum at Dealey Plaza opened to the public in February 1989.

Collections at The Sixth Floor Museum today include a wide variety of objects, images and documents related to the Kennedy assassination.

"I've never been back here to Dealey Plaza in forty years, and so you're kind of overwhelmed by it. But I was taken by the fact that here on this rainy day during the week, so many people are here. I find that fascinating that this is happening. And some 400,000 people a year visit this Museum. I think they ought to—to see how our president was murdered and where it happened. And I think Dallas, to its credit, has come to grips with this."

—Jack Valenti
Special Assistant to President Lyndon Johnson
2004

The Texas School Book Depository and Dealey Plaza just after the assassination in 1963.

These images show crowds in Dealey Plaza on different anniversaries of the assassination throughout the years.

Known today as the Dallas County Administration Building, this is how the former Texas School Book Depository looks 50 years after the assassination.

THE SIXTH FLOOR MUSEUM TODAY

The Sixth Floor Museum at Dealey Plaza serves as a repository for more than 40,000 historical items related to President Kennedy, his assassination and its aftermath, the city of Dallas and the early 1960s. Included in the Museum's holdings is a rich collection of oral histories from eyewitnesses, law enforcement officials, community leaders, White House officials and news media. The Museum actively continues to seek participants for the Oral History Project and invites anyone with recollections of President Kennedy, the assassination or other historic events of that time to contribute.

Most of the first-hand accounts in the Museum's collections can be viewed in the Museum's Reading Room. Free by appointment, the Reading Room also provides researchers, students, teachers and history enthusiasts with a portal to the Museum's vast collection and over 5,000 books, magazines, newspapers and films.

Living History presentations, traveling exhibitions, special events and engaging programs are presented on the Museum's seventh floor. The Museum Bookstore, located in the Visitors Center, offers books and media, a selection of prints and posters and a variety of collectible souvenirs. The Museum Store + Café, across the street from the Museum at the corner of Elm and Houston, features an expanded assortment of gift items that reflect the pop culture of the 1960s and our Texas heritage. A selection of freshly brewed coffees and teas, sandwiches and snacks can be found in the Café, all in a historical setting that's perfect for reflecting upon your visit and President Kennedy's life and legacy.

The 1960 Campaign

KENNEDY
FOR PRESIDENT

JOHNSON
FOR VICE PRESIDENT

PRESIDENT KENNEDY'S LEGACY

President Kennedy represents many things to many people: an emblem of the civil rights movements of the 1960s; founder of the Peace Corps; the inspiration behind America's conquest of space; the beginning of America's involvement in Vietnam; a proponent of education, arts and culture; a great speaker; a cultural icon and one of America's favorite leaders. His assassination had a profound effect on millions of people at home and abroad. However, both his death and his legacy remain open to interpretation.

Historians have debated whether Kennedy's death fostered national unrest during the later 1960s and 1970s. Undoubtedly the assassination helped shape John F. Kennedy as a legend in popular culture. National opinion polls have consistently named him one of the greatest American presidents in history. He remains a positive force in the collective memory, a memory that has passed to new generations that never knew him. John F. Kennedy endures as a symbol of commitment and the ability to effect change. These symbolic values may ultimately outlast the search for historical certainties.

Press release detailing President Johnson's first address to Congress on November 27, 1963.

"Today John Fitzgerald Kennedy lives on in the immortal words and works that he left behind…

No words are sad enough to express our sense of loss. No words are strong enough to express our determination to continue the forward thrust of America that he began.

The dream of conquering the vastness of space… the dream of a Peace Corps in less-developed nations – the dream of education for all of our children – the dream of jobs for all who seek them and need them – the dream of care for our elderly – the dream of an all-out attack on mental illness – and above all the dream of equal rights for all Americans, whatever their race or color – these and other American dreams have been vitalized by his drive and by his dedication."

—*President Lyndon B. Johnson*
Address to Congress
November 27, 1963

"Mankind must put an end to war—or war will put an end to mankind….Let us call a truce to terror. Let us invoke the blessings of peace."

—*President John F. Kennedy*
Address to the United Nations
September 25, 1961

"I urge this generation of Americans, who are the fathers and mothers of 350 million Americans who will live in this country in the year 2000, and I want those Americans who live here in 2000 to feel that those of us who had positions of responsibility in the Sixties did our part...."

—President John F. Kennedy
High School Memorial Stadium
Great Falls, Montana
September 26, 1963

"There was really a kind of excitement, intellectual depth, and challenge from Kennedy, that we felt part of that Kennedy generation. So there was deep, deep grief over the loss of this young vigorous president who we felt maybe would take the country in a new and dynamic direction."

—The Reverend Richard Deats
Social rights activist
2006

"...the eyes of the world now look into space, to the moon and to the planets beyond, and we have vowed that we shall not see it governed by a hostile flag of conquest, but by a banner of freedom and peace."

—President John F. Kennedy
Rice University
Houston, TX
September 12, 1962

President Kennedy and Friendship 7, the spacecraft in which astronaut John Glenn splashed down into the ocean after becoming the first American to orbit the Earth.

JOHN F. KENNEDY MEMORIAL PLAZA

Designed by American architect Philip Johnson, the John F. Kennedy Memorial is located one block east of Dealey Plaza. Johnson designed the memorial as a cenotaph, or "open tomb," to symbolize the freedom of President Kennedy's spirit. Dedicated on June 24, 1970, the memorial is a square, roofless room, 30 feet high and 50 by 50 feet wide. It is built of 72 white pre-cast concrete columns, most of which seem to float with no visible support 29 inches above the ground. John Fitzgerald Kennedy's name carved in gold upon granite provides the only verbal message in the empty space.

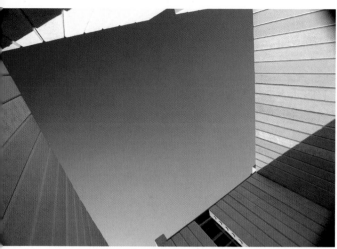

"…a place of quiet refuge, an enclosed place of thought and contemplation separated from the city around, but near the sky and earth."

—Philip Johnson
Architect
The Rededication of the John Fitzgerald Kennedy Memorial
June 24, 2000

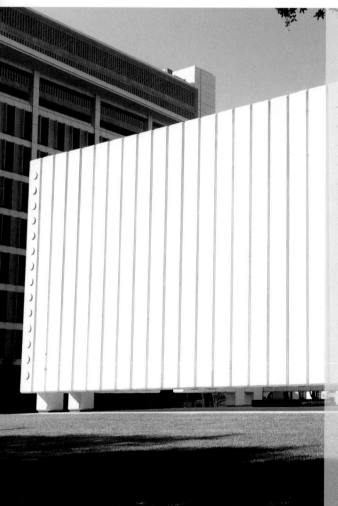

"The joy and excitement of John Fitzgerald Kennedy's life belonged to all men. So did the pain and sorrow of his death. When he died on November 22, 1963, shock and agony touched human conscience throughout the world. In Dallas, Texas, there was a special sorrow. The young President died in Dallas. The death bullets were fired 200 yards west of this site. This memorial, designed by Philip Johnson, was erected by the people of Dallas. Thousands of citizens contributed support, money and effort. It is not a memorial to the pain and sorrow of death, but stands as a permanent tribute to the joy and excitement of one man's life.

John Fitzgerald Kennedy's life."

—Inscription on a granite marker in the
John F. Kennedy Memorial Plaza

61

"History, after all, is the memory of a nation."

—*President John F. Kennedy*
Introduction American Heritage Illustrated History of the United States
1963

62

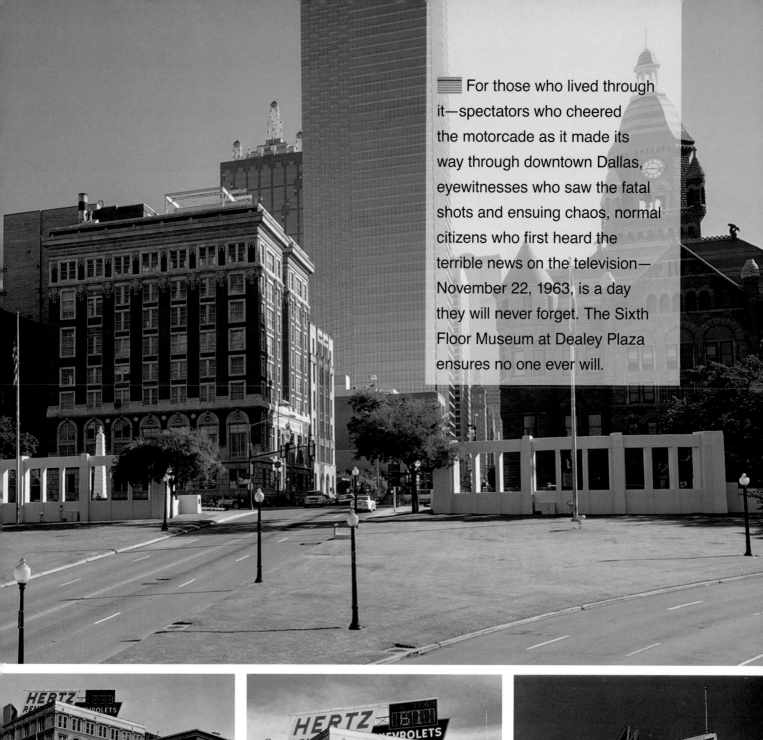

For those who lived through it—spectators who cheered the motorcade as it made its way through downtown Dallas, eyewitnesses who saw the fatal shots and ensuing chaos, normal citizens who first heard the terrible news on the television—November 22, 1963, is a day they will never forget. The Sixth Floor Museum at Dealey Plaza ensures no one ever will.

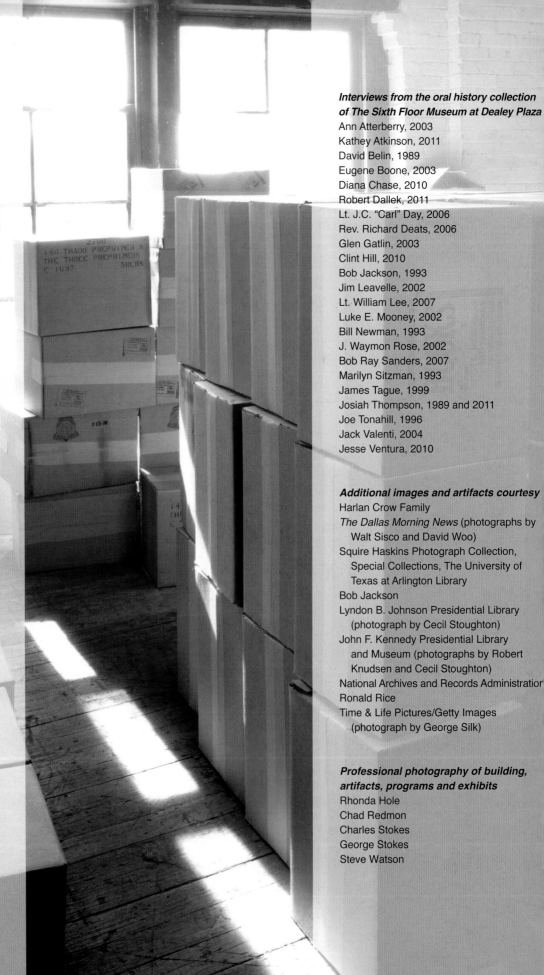

CREDITS

From the image and media collections of The Sixth Floor Museum at Dealey Plaza

Roy Botello Collection
Claire Campbell Collection
Gregory Clock Collection (photograph by Frank Muto)
William E. Cooper Collection (photograph by Walter de Lima Meyers)
Dallas County Sheriff's Department Collection
Dallas Times Herald Collection (photographs by William Allen, William Beal, Darryl Heikes, Bob Jackson, Eamon Kennedy, Al Volkland and unidentified)
Lt. J. C. "Carl" Day Collection
Tom C. Dillard Collection, *The Dallas Morning News*
Institutional archives
George Jefferies Collection
Spaulding Jones Collection
KRLD/KDFW-TV Collection
R. W. "Rusty" Livingston Collection (Dallas Police Department photographs)
Dorothy and Carter Murphy Collection
Chester and Arlene Mzyk Collection
Joseph O'Dwyer Collection
George Reid Collection
Robert Russell Collection
Lyndal L. Shaneyfelt Collection
Jay Skaggs Collection
Jack A. Titus Collection
Jim Walker Collection
WFAA-TV Collection
Robert L. White Collection
Phil Willis Collection
Bill Winfrey Collection
Zapruder Family Collection

From the artifact collections of The Sixth Floor Museum at Dealey Plaza

Kent Barker Collection
Darlene Bush Collection
Alex Guofeng Cao Collection
Vivian Castleberry Collection
Lt. J. C. "Carl" Day Collection
Joe M. Dealey Jr. Collection
Elsie Dorman Collection
David and Susan Hall Collection
Nancy Hamilton Collection
Cheryl Hartman Collection
William F. Lee Collection
R. W. "Rusty" Livingston Collection
Ruth Marble Collection
Mel McCoy Collection
Luke E. Mooney Collection
Anthony Pugliese Collection
Skipper and Joel Sanders Collection
The Sixth Floor Museum at Dealey Plaza Collection
Bernadine Stetzel Collection
Kathleen Morrow Whatley Collection

Interviews from the oral history collection of The Sixth Floor Museum at Dealey Plaza

Ann Atterberry, 2003
Kathey Atkinson, 2011
David Belin, 1989
Eugene Boone, 2003
Diana Chase, 2010
Robert Dallek, 2011
Lt. J.C. "Carl" Day, 2006
Rev. Richard Deats, 2006
Glen Gatlin, 2003
Clint Hill, 2010
Bob Jackson, 1993
Jim Leavelle, 2002
Lt. William Lee, 2007
Luke E. Mooney, 2002
Bill Newman, 1993
J. Waymon Rose, 2002
Bob Ray Sanders, 2007
Marilyn Sitzman, 1993
James Tague, 1999
Josiah Thompson, 1989 and 2011
Joe Tonahill, 1996
Jack Valenti, 2004
Jesse Ventura, 2010

Additional images and artifacts courtesy

Harlan Crow Family
The Dallas Morning News (photographs by Walt Sisco and David Woo)
Squire Haskins Photograph Collection, Special Collections, The University of Texas at Arlington Library
Bob Jackson
Lyndon B. Johnson Presidential Library (photograph by Cecil Stoughton)
John F. Kennedy Presidential Library and Museum (photographs by Robert Knudsen and Cecil Stoughton)
National Archives and Records Administration
Ronald Rice
Time & Life Pictures/Getty Images (photograph by George Silk)

Professional photography of building, artifacts, programs and exhibits

Rhonda Hole
Chad Redmon
Charles Stokes
George Stokes
Steve Watson

Terry Fox

A STORY OF HOPE

by Maxine Trottier

Scholastic Canada Ltd.
Toronto New York London Auckland Sydney
Mexico City New Delhi Hong Kong Buenos Aires

For Kelly Doig, our fighter.
— M.T.

Scholastic Canada Ltd.
604 King Street West, Toronto, Ontario M5V 1E1, Canada
Scholastic Inc.
557 Broadway, New York, NY 10012, USA
Scholastic Australia Pty Limited
PO Box 579, Gosford, NSW 2250, Australia
Scholastic New Zealand Limited
Private Bag 94407, Botany, Manukau 2163, New Zealand
Scholastic Children's Books
Euston House, 24 Eversholt Street, London NW1 1DB, UK

www.scholastic.ca

Library and Archives Canada Cataloguing in Publication
Trottier, Maxine
Terry Fox : a story of hope / by Maxine Trottier.

ISBN 978-1-4431-0250-6

1. Fox, Terry, 1958-1981--Juvenile literature.
2. Cancer--Patients--Biography--Juvenile literature.
3. Runners (Sports)--Canada--Biography--Juvenile
literature. I. Title.

RC265.6.F68T76 2010   j362.196'994'0092   C2010-900181-8

8 7 6 5 4   Printed in Malaysia   108   16 17 18 19 20

Terry loved children. From his experiences with cancer, he knew they were far more courageous than he was, that they never gave up and always found a way to smile. This book is dedicated to those children who truly defined hope, and to the kids who cheered Terry on from St. John's, Newfoundland, to Thunder Bay, Ontario. It is dedicated to the children of those children who will read this story. Terry learned to dream big from kids just like you. Never doubt his words: "Anything is possible if you try. Dreams are made if people try."

— *Darrell Fox, August, 2005*

The Marathon of Hope

April 12, 1980 — September 1, 1980

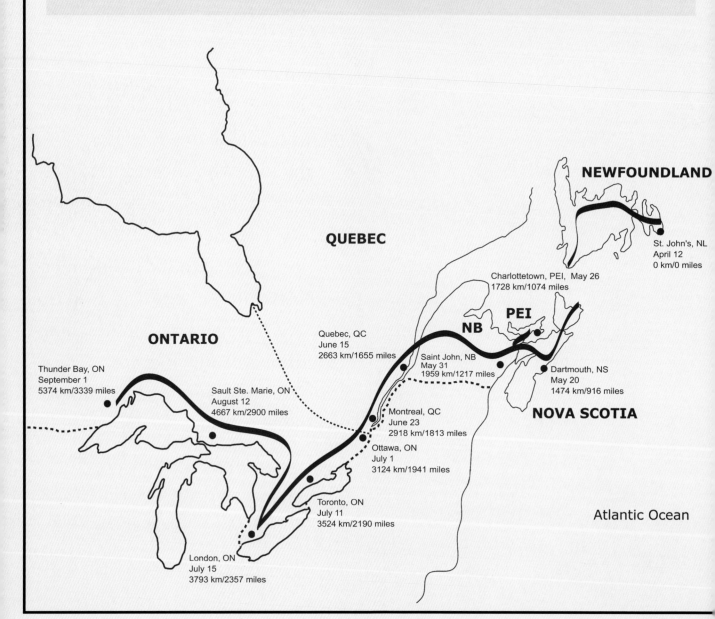

NEWFOUNDLAND

QUEBEC

St. John's, NL
April 12
0 km/0 miles

Charlottetown, PEI, May 26
1728 km/1074 miles

PEI

NB

ONTARIO

Quebec, QC
June 15
2663 km/1655 miles

Saint John, NB
May 31
1959 km/1217 miles

Dartmouth, NS
May 20
1474 km/916 miles

Thunder Bay, ON
September 1
5374 km/3339 miles

Sault Ste. Marie, ON
August 12
4667 km/2900 miles

Montreal, QC
June 23
2918 km/1813 miles

NOVA SCOTIA

Ottawa, ON
July 1
3124 km/1941 miles

Toronto, ON
July 11
3524 km/2190 miles

Atlantic Ocean

London, ON
July 15
3793 km/2357 miles

Hope is a quiet thing. It is about believing in a dream, no matter how long and hard the road may be. Hope is a young man running across Canada to help find a cure for a disease that had caused so much hurting. It is the echo of his footsteps pounding on a lonely stretch of highway just before dawn. Hope is the story of Terry Fox.

"Mom, I'm going to run across Canada."

1

9 MONTHS OLD

Terry Fox was born on July 28, 1958, in Winnipeg, Manitoba. This picture of him at 9 months was taken in front of the Fox home on Gertrude Avenue. Terry would grow into a determined boy, who even as a toddler showed the persistence with which he would face life's challenges.

It all began in a very ordinary way when Rolly and Betty Fox's son Terry was born. Patiently stacking and restacking his blocks, playing with toy soldiers — these things were a part of Terry's childhood. He built snowmen with his younger brother, Darrell, during the harsh Winnipeg winters and watched his baby sister, Judith, toddle around the house. There were family picnics and walks to school with his older brother, Fred.

2

Wearing their matching sweaters and pants made by their Grandma Wark, four-year-old Terry (right) and his brother Fred pose in front of the tree on Christmas morning.

Winnipeg, Man.
Novemeber 29, 1964

Dear Santa Claus,
For Christmas I would like you to bring me a Battleground play set t a Johnny Seven gun.
My little brother Darrell would like a train pull toy.
Merry Christmas to you.
My address is 27 Camrose Bay
Thank You
Terry Fox

Even at the age of six, Terry's letter to Santa Claus, printed by his mom, shows that he thought not only of himself, but of his little brother.

A formal portrait of the smiling Fox family. Clockwise from left: 10-year-old Terry, Rolly, Fred (11 ½), Darrell (6), Judith (3), and Betty in the centre. Terry's mother worked as a homemaker; later on she would work part-time in a card shop. His father was a Canadian National Railway switchman.

3

Each year the Fox kids dressed up and had their portraits done by a photographer. Here, Terry is 10 years old.

Terry pitches to his mom at a local park. Fred is the catcher.

The Fox kids; Terry is on the right. By now the family lived in Port Coquitlam. The kids all loved to play for hours in the huge field behind their house on Morrill Street. Another favourite spot was the Coquitlam River. Terry walked to school and went home for lunch each day; he loved bread and jam.

4

Terry's grade eight Mary Hill school identification card from 1971-1972, the year that he became friends with a classmate named Doug Alward. The two shy, slightly built boys shared a love of biology and competitive sports.

In a pre-Christmas snapshot taken by Rolly in 1973, the rest of the Fox family stands in front of the fireplace in their living room. Terry is on the far right.

"I like challenges. I don't give up."

Then came a move to British Columbia. Port Coquitlam was the perfect place for the Fox kids to grow up. For Terry, there was roughhousing with his father and brothers and summer jobs picking blueberries, saving the money to buy his own clothes, a bike or school supplies. There were quiet times as well, when he would play alone for hours. School meant more than hard work; it meant new friends. One boy, Doug Alward, began a friendship with Terry that would endure for a lifetime.

Nine-year-old Terry, standing in the family's backyard, proudly holds a trophy won while playing baseball with his team, the Braves. Terry was a pitcher, catcher and first baseman.

Terry loved all sorts of sports. Here he is with his peewee soccer team, in 1971 in Port Coquitlam. Terry is third from the right, and Doug Alward stands next to him, behind the player with the ball.

And there were sports.

Terry played soccer, baseball and rugby. He competed in track and field and took up cross-country running, but what he wanted to do more than anything else was to play basketball. Terry was terrible at the game, yet he wouldn't give up his dream. All through the summer before grade nine, he played one-on-one with Doug. That fall, Terry ran to school each morning and stayed late after classes so that he could practise. The Fox stubbornness paid off. By grade ten, Terry had earned a place on the

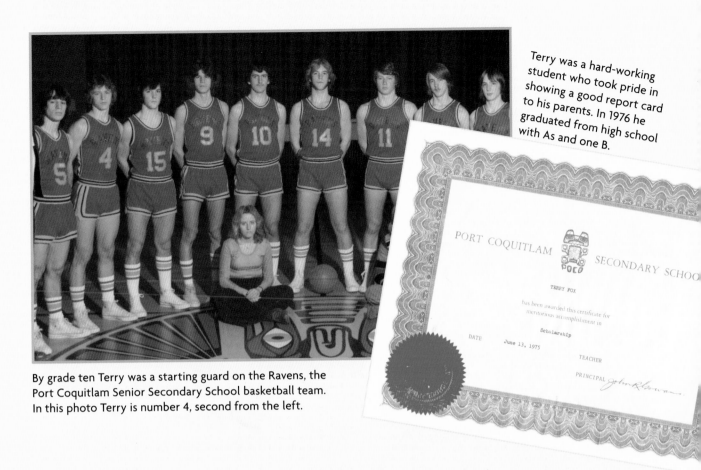

PORT COQUITLAM   SECONDARY SCHOOL

POCO

TERRY FOX

has been awarded this certificate for meritorious accomplishment in

Scholarship

DATE   June 13, 1975

TEACHER

PRINCIPAL *John R Bowman*

By grade ten Terry was a starting guard on the Ravens, the Port Coquitlam Senior Secondary School basketball team. In this photo Terry is number 4, second from the left.

school basketball team, and when he and Doug graduated, they shared the Athlete of the Year Award. Terry enrolled at university and, more competitive than ever, he made the basketball team there. He had plans. Eventually he hoped to become a high school Phys Ed teacher. His future looked bright. Life was good.

"Mom and Dad didn't like me getting up early to go to school to play basketball ... I'd run in the dark with all my books and clothes flying."

Terry's student ID from SFU.

The track and pool complex at Simon Fraser University, where Terry enrolled in the fall of 1976 to study kinesiology. Ever the athlete, he made the junior varsity basketball team there.

Judith, Terry and their mother at home, Christmas 1976. Terry and Judith are playing a game of "Operation."

Later, Terry relaxes in the front room with his sore leg extended.

Then, in November of 1976, Terry began having pain in his right knee. He tried to ignore it and continued to play basketball, but by March the pain was unbearable. His father drove him to the hospital where Terry had X-rays and a bone scan. With his family around him, he was told the results of the tests. He had bone cancer. His leg would have to be amputated as soon as possible. In an instant, Terry's life was changed forever.

At first, he cried at the thought of what had happened, at what faced him, but Terry pulled himself together. This was just one more challenge. He had worked hard before to achieve his goals and he could do it again, even if it meant doing it with only one leg. He wouldn't let anyone pity him, any more than he would pity himself.

Terry's fight with cancer had begun.

"Nobody is ever going to call me a quitter."

Terry was 18 years old when he was diagnosed with a type of cancer called osteogenic sarcoma and had his leg amputated. Within a month of his surgery, Terry was at home and walking using a temporary prosthesis with the help of crutches. He wouldn't need those crutches for long.

Terry's prosthesis with its straps and gears was made of steel and fibreglass. He would run two thirds of the way across Canada using this artificial leg.

Six days later, his leg was amputated and within a few incredible weeks he was learning to walk wearing a temporary prosthesis. He began chemotherapy at the cancer clinic. For Terry, those were difficult months. The suffering he saw there moved him deeply. When his treatment was finished, Terry left the hospital a changed person. He believed that he now had a debt to pay, that he would live his life to give courage to people who had been stricken by cancer. On the night before his surgery, he had read about an amputee runner,

The *Runner's World* article in which Terry read about Dick Traum, a one-legged runner in the New York City Marathon. "I was lying in bed looking at this magazine, thinking if he can do it, I can do it, too."

a man who had run the New York City Marathon. It had filled him not only with admiration, but with hope. He now had a new dream, one that for the time being he kept to himself.

Terry Fox had decided that someday he would run across Canada to raise money for cancer research.

"That's the thing about cancer. I'm not the only one. It happens all the time to people."

Terry endured 16 months of chemotherapy. His hair fell out and he often felt weak and nauseated. During this time Rick Hansen asked him to play wheelchair basketball, and he eagerly rose to the challenge. In this image taken from a home movie, Terry shoots a basket in the SFU gym.

Terry receives the 1978 Canadian championship trophy for wheelchair basketball on behalf of his team, the Vancouver Cablecars.

On August 30, 1979, Terry headed to northern B.C. with Doug, Darrell and some friends to compete in the Prince George to Boston Marathon, a 17-mile race. He finished with a time of three hours and nine minutes, only ten minutes behind the last two-legged runner.

He began to train. Playing wheelchair basketball strengthened his upper body as well as his spirit. Running came next. Pushing himself a little farther each time, he built up his endurance and increased his strength. The day that he ran an entire mile was an enormous triumph for him. A double step with his left leg and a stride with his artificial leg. Over and over and over again. The prosthesis rubbed his stump raw and bloody, his bones were bruised, his foot blistered badly and he lost toenails, but he wouldn't give up. When Terry ran his first and only long-distance race, although he finished last, he finished. It was the biggest day of his life. Now he knew he could run across Canada.

"I broke it down. Get that mile down, get to that sign, get past the corner and around that bend... That's all I thought about."

Terry began writing heartfelt letters asking for support. He trained harder than ever, toughening himself for what was to come, ignoring the pain, making his plans, never losing sight of his dream. For months he continued to run around tracks, along roads, up and down hills, covering more than 3000 miles altogether. Finally he was ready.

Part of Terry's first letter, written with the help of his friend Rika Noda. Betty Fox helped Terry send other letters as well, to the Ford Motor Company, Imperial Oil, Adidas and other companies. They agreed to provide a van, fuel, shoes, food vouchers and money for the run. Although Terry appreciated the support, he steadfastly refused to endorse any business. He even insisted on wearing only clothing without logos.

I was rudely awakened by the feelings that surrounded and coursed through the cancer clinic....I could not leave knowing these faces and feelings would still exist. Somewhere the hurting must stop... and I was determined to take myself to the limit for this cause.

I feel strong not only physically, but more important, emotionally. Soon I will be adding one full mile a week, and coupled with weight training I have been doing, by next April I will be ready to achieve something that for me was once only a distant dream reserved for the world of miracles - to run across Canada to raise money for the fight against cancer.

The running I can do, even if I have to crawl every last mile. We need your help. The people in cancer clinics all over the world need people who believe in miracles.

Terry Fox, October 1979

14

"Somewhere the hurting must stop ... I was determined to take myself to the limit for this cause."

While Terry ran, he counted telephone poles to help himself forget the pain in his foot and stump. He calculated his runs in miles; metric measurement had just become official in Canada in 1977. With one mile equalling 1.6 kilometres, Terry ran a total of 5084 kilometres during his training.

On the morning of April 12, 1980, Terry brought two empty glass jugs to Newfoundland's shore to fill with Atlantic sea water. One jug he planned to pour into the Pacific Ocean at the end of the marathon, the other he would keep as a souvenir. But the waves washed away one of the jugs. The one that he did fill sits in his parents' home today. With Doug Alward and a small crowd watching, Terry bent down to touch the stones and then dipped his leg in the harbour at the foot of Temperance Street in St. John's. He climbed the steep, gravelled hill to the road. The Marathon of Hope had begun.

If you had been in St. John's, Newfoundland, on that cold and windy day in April of 1980, you would have seen a young man dip his artificial leg into the Atlantic Ocean. You would have seen Terry Fox set out. You would have witnessed the beginning of an amazing journey: the Marathon of Hope.

Terry's postcard sent home to his mom, dad and Judith, postmarked Moncton, NB, May 30, 1980. It reads: "Hello, hope you are fine. Well I have made it to Charlottetown, P.E.I. Most beautiful country so far. People greeted me and followed me in from ten miles out of the city. Newfoundland's up to $40,000 now! Terry"

"I'm trying to raise as much money as I can."

Terry's friend Doug drove the van that had been donated for the run. In it was their gear, food and running shoes, three spare legs and some parts for repairs. Day after day, no matter what the weather, no matter how he felt, Terry ran. One mile at a time, with Doug waiting in the van up ahead, Terry pushed himself through Newfoundland and Nova Scotia. It wasn't easy, but each step was bringing him closer to the west coast of Canada, closer to home, closer to beating cancer. On he ran, from dawn until dusk, through Prince Edward Island and then New Brunswick, where his brother Darrell joined them. Into Quebec and then on to Ontario. The miles and the donations increased.

Terry's postcard home to Judith and his parents, postmarked Fredericton, NB, June 4, 1980. In it he talks about the "bucket," the fibreglass sleeve in which his stump sat:
"Hello! Hope you are fine. Great to have Darrell here. I'm having a tough week. Bucket isn't fitting right. Pain! 15 miles short of Fredericton now. Hope to get it fixed here. Terry"

Doug drives the van behind Terry as he runs. Until they reached Ontario and Terry was assigned a police escort, it was Doug and Darrell, 17, who looked out for Terry's safety on the road. Each day was tough. Enormous meals of pancakes, hamburgers, fries, beans and rice gave Terry energy and fuelled his body. The money he was raising fuelled his spirit.

"Some days it was so hard to get going; sometimes it was all pain."

Terry ran into Montreal, Quebec, wearing the French version of his Marathon of Hope T-shirt.

Terry ran an average of 26 miles a day, the equivalent of a marathon, for 143 days. With Doug driving the van, Darrell would gamely zigzag through traffic taking donations from passing motorists.

Terry runs along University Avenue in Toronto. He tried to acknowledge the thousands of people who came out to see him with a lift of his hand, what Darrell called a "Terry wave."

Terry didn't just run. During his months on the road he gave dozens of speeches, made endless phone calls, attended receptions and gave interviews. It was exhausting, but it did help raise money. At Toronto's Nathan Phillips Square, Maple Leafs captain Darryl Sittler presented Terry with his 1980 NHL All-Star team sweater. On that day Terry raised 100,000 dollars. He ran on, through the muggy summer weather, south to London and then back north. On July 28, Terry ran into Gravenhurst where he was welcomed with a 22nd birthday celebration.

So did the enthusiasm and warmth of Canadians everywhere. People cheered, urging Terry on with banners and signs. Some wept when they saw him pass by, his face a mask of concentration, while others stood in silence, touched by his courage and his cause. The eyes of the country were on a young man whose every step said that cancer could be beaten, that there was hope. He didn't care about being famous. He wasn't keeping a penny of the money being raised. One dollar was all he asked from each Canadian. One dollar. Terry Fox was running all the way across Canada, and he was going to make it. He had never been happier.

"If you've given a dollar, you are part of the Marathon of Hope."

On August 27, Terry had a rare opportunity to relax. Here he has just been swimming with a fellow amputee, 10-year-old Greg Scott, in Jackfish Lake, not far from Thunder Bay.

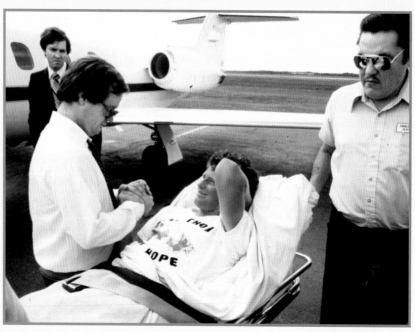

On September 2, Terry lies strapped on a stretcher waiting to be lifted into the small jet that would fly him, along with his parents, home to British Columbia for more treatment. He is talking to Bill Vigars, who worked for the Ontario division of the Canadian Cancer Society. Vigars had travelled with Terry and scheduled his appearances in Ontario. Like everyone else, he was stunned by the return of Terry's cancer.

But just outside of Thunder Bay, Ontario, the coughing and chest pain began. Terry asked Doug to drive him to a hospital. Before any tests were done, Terry was certain of what they would show.

He was right; the cancer had returned. Now it was in his lungs.

" . . . I began to think . . . there's something wrong. This may be the last mile."

Back in New Westminster, B.C., the same day, Terry, his mother and his father give a press conference at the Royal Columbian Hospital. In spite of the fact that Darryl Sittler, the Toronto Maple Leafs and the NHL offered to finish the run for him, Terry told the world he would do it himself someday.

With his parents at his side, Terry broke the news to the rest of Canada at a press conference. The nation was stunned. He had run 3339 miles in just 143 days, and it all seemed so unfair. Terry, though, knew that cancer had nothing to do with fairness. He knew that what was happening to him could happen to anyone, and that now people would understand exactly what having cancer meant. Terry had done his best to run across Canada; he would do his best to fight this cancer and some day finish the run.

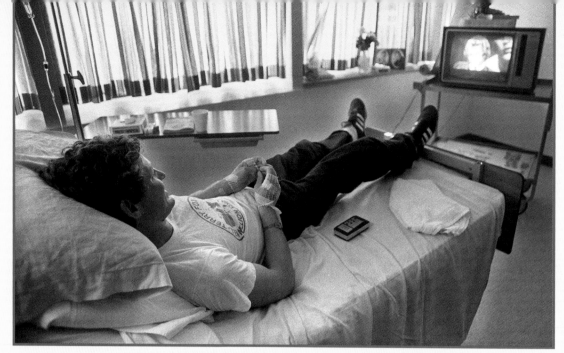

On September 7, 1980, Terry, who is undergoing more chemotherapy, lies in hospital wearing his Marathon of Hope T-shirt. He is watching a CTV fundraising broadcast that raised 10.5 million dollars for cancer research.

Buttons such as this one were a way that people demonstrated their involvement with Terry and the Marathon of Hope.

Young people were huge supporters of Terry during his run. They stuck by him and continued to raise money while he fought the return of cancer.

Terry met Isadore Sharp when he ran through Montreal. Sharp, a Montreal philanthropist whose teenaged son had died of cancer, was responsible for organizing a fundraiser among the businessmen in his city. Its motto was, "Let's Make Terry's Run Really Count." Later Sharp assured Terry that an annual run would be held in his name. Sharp still serves as a Director of the Terry Fox Foundation.

Terry's words shook our country. While he endured yet more chemotherapy, Canadians everywhere began to raise money. There was a telethon. There were walk-a-thons, run-a-thons, dances and recitals. Corporations donated huge sums, and children sold lemonade. By February, 1981, Terry's run and the generosity it had inspired had raised more than 24 million dollars, just as he had dreamed it would.

"We're really going to have to try hard in order to beat it, try harder than we ever have before."

Terry sits at home after attending a special ceremony on September 18, 1980, in which he became a Companion of the Order of Canada. He remains the youngest person to have received the honour. On October 21, he was awarded the Order of the Dogwood, B.C.'s highest civilian award. Since his death, schools across Canada, parks, an icebreaker and even a mountain in B.C. have been named after him.

Terry was showered with honours. Thousands of letters and telegrams of encouragement from Canada and all around the world poured into his hospital room and into the Foxes' home. People were still saying that they were behind him, that he shouldn't give up, that he could make it. Terry tried to beat the cancer. He fought harder than he had ever fought before, but some things are simply not meant to be, no matter how much we want them. Surrounded by his family, Terry died on June 28, 1981, just before dawn, the still and peaceful time when he most loved to run.

"Even if I don't finish, we need others to continue. It's got to keep going without me."

Terry's funeral on July 2, 1981, brought the country together in mourning. He was laid to rest in the Port Coquitlam Cemetery, not far from his favourite lookout, a quiet place where he sometimes went to think. Monuments honouring Terry can be seen in St. John's, Newfoundland, in Port Coquitlam and Vancouver, B.C., and in Ottawa. This one stands in Thunder Bay, Ontario.

Hope is a quiet thing, but if a dream is strong enough, hope can grow and grow until it touches everyone. Terry Fox's Marathon of Hope did not end on that morning. People are still running with his dream, people who believe in miracles, people who share Terry's certainty that anything is possible if you try. And because Terry Fox tried his best, because he ran his marathon and gave us his precious gift of hope, someday a cure for cancer will be found.

Someday the hurting will stop.

On April 4, 2005, the Royal Canadian Mint released a one-dollar coin with Terry's image on it, in honour of the 25th anniversary of his Marathon of Hope.

"Even though I'm not running anymore, we still have to try to find a cure for cancer. Other people should go ahead and try to do their own thing now."

Students parade down Main Street in Humboldt, Saskatchewan in September, 2004, to promote the annual Terry Fox Run.

Before Terry Fox died, he knew that an event would be held to continue his efforts to raise money for the fight against cancer. As Isadore Sharp had promised, the Terry Fox Run was established to carry on his Marathon of Hope. Held for the first time in 1981, it drew 300,000 participants across Canada, who walked, wheeled and ran to raise 3.5 million dollars for the cause.

In Canada, the Terry Fox Run has been held each September since then, usually on the second Sunday after Labour Day. There is no entry fee and there are no prizes. Families, organizations, schools and individuals come together in a non-competitive event, with the help of thousands of volunteers, to keep Terry's dream of hope alive. Terry Fox Runs have spread throughout the world, to places like India and Ireland, Cuba and China. The Terry Fox Foundation was established in 1988 as an independent non-profit organization to distribute the funds raised for cancer research in Terry's name.

When Terry Fox took the first step in his Marathon of Hope, he was encouraged by his family, friends and supporters, of course, but he alone was making the tremendous effort to run across Canada. Few people saw his first step, but after he had run thousands of miles and taken millions of steps, all of Canada was inspired by his courage. And the inspiration did not end with his death. Instead, as time has passed, it has increased.

The Terry Fox Foundation talks about "a single dream, a world of hope." It is not only raising millions for research, it is keeping Terry's story alive, sharing it with adults and, perhaps more importantly, with young people. In 2005, for the 25th anniversary of the Marathon of Hope, the first Terry Fox National School Run Day was held. More than 3 million students from 9000 schools participated. Since then, millions more have joined in, and Run Day has become a yearly event for schools in every Canadian province and territory, as young people carry on what Terry began. That same year, in the largest Run event ever held, 14,000 people ran or walked the 12.9 kilometres across Confederation Bridge, which links New Brunswick and Prince Edward Island. Through their efforts, $375,000 was raised in Terry's name.

The event was so successful that plans were made to repeat it for the Marathon of Hope's 30th anniversary.

In 2007 the first Terry Fox Works Day took place. Just as the school runs were created for students, now co-workers could join together to raise money for cancer research. Some businesses organized bake sales or auctions. Some workplaces had Dress-down Fridays, special breakfasts or theme days. It was the beginning of The Great Canadian Head Shave, a tribute to honour all the cancer patients who undergo chemotherapy and suffer hair loss. To launch the event, Terry's parents, brothers and sister cheerfully allowed their own heads to be shaved clean to raise money for the Foundation. In 2010 it became The Great Canadian Hair "Do," with many

ways to participate — all in the name of fundraising, and all filled with the spirit of fun.

Terry always looked to the future with great hope — to a future that would be cancer-free if everyone played a part. With that in mind, the Terry Fox Foundation launched the Terry Fox Research Institute — or TFRI

— in October of 2007. Its purpose is to provide funds to support research projects in which cancer researchers and physicians work together. For example, in 2008 the TFRI joined with the Canadian Partnership Against Cancer to begin a national, early lung cancer detection study. It has helped to save the lives of people whose cancers might otherwise have been discovered too late.

Terry understood that cancer touches the entire world. Today, International Runs take place in dozens of countries. They are organized by Canadian armed forces personnel, by Canadian embassy or consulate workers, or by individuals who have simply been moved to help. Not a single Terry Fox event has ever included any entrance fee, prizes or first place medals, yet everyone is a winner. Everyone shares in the success. Over the years, Terry's cause has brought people together in a fight against cancer that has raised close to 500 million dollars.

In 1980 Adidas had provided shoes for Terry's cross-country run. He used nine pairs of them, wearing out the left shoe of each pair. For years one of Terry's famous shoes has been on display at the Bata Shoe Museum in Toronto. But then along came an opportunity for people to own a similar pair. For the 25th anniversary of the Marathon of Hope, Adidas created 6600 replica pairs for the Terry Fox Foundation. The shoes sold out in less than a week, with more than half a million dollars raised for cancer research. Two years later, the Foundation auctioned off 12 extra-special pairs of the shoes. Each stripe on each pair had been signed by a great athlete — 12 in total, including Wayne Gretzky, Catriona Le May Doan, Kurt Browning and Sidney Crosby — all of

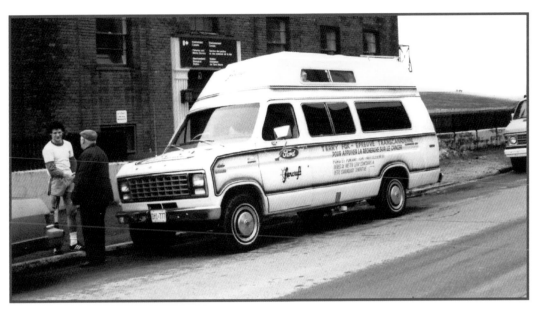

whom were honoured to be part of the project. The bidding was keen, with the shoes going at an average of $4000 a pair.

In September of 1980, the van that accompanied Terry on his run had been left in Thunder Bay when he had to fly back to British Columbia to continue his fight with cancer. The Fox family sometimes wondered what had happened to that van, but it was not until 2006 that the mystery was solved. The Ford Motor Company of Canada, which had lent the van to Terry, had long since sold it. The van ended up in East Vancouver, where it was being used by a rock band as a touring bus. When Darrell Fox finally saw it again, memories of the Marathon of Hope flooded back. After all, the van had been their home for 183 days. It had been Terry's sanctuary. The family

bought the van, Ford restored it, and on May 22, 2008, it was unveiled at St. John's, Newfoundland. From there it made a cross-Canada fundraising journey for cancer research, eventually arriving in Vancouver.

Many awards have been given to Terry Fox, both before and after his death. In 1980 he was made a Companion of the Order of Canada, and received British Columbia's highest honour and the American Cancer Society's Sword of Hope. In the fall of the next year, he was posthumously inducted into the Canadian Sports Hall of Fame. Schools, buildings, roads, parks, a ship and a mountain now bear his name. From coast to coast, statues and memorials stand in recognition of what he accomplished. He was voted Canada's Greatest Hero in 1999, and declared a National Historic Person in 2008.

Many Terry Fox awards have been created, to be presented to those who live up to the ideals in which he believed. In 1981, Simon Fraser University made Terry the first recipient of The Terry Fox Gold Medal, an award presented annually to a student who shows true courage in difficult times, just as Terry did. The Canadian government created the Terry Fox Humanitarian Award, which provides scholarships to individuals whose high standards are shown not only in their studies but in what they do for their communities.

What Terry stood for echoes through it all.

Terry Fox's memory was further honoured during the Vancouver 2010 Winter Olympics. His father, Rolly, was a torchbearer on the final leg through the city, and his mother, Betty, proudly helped to carry in the Olympic flag

at the opening ceremonies. As the Games drew to a close, Terry's parents presented the Vancouver 2010 Terry Fox Award. Created to honour the athlete who showed the same spirit of courage and humility that their son had, it was shared by bronze medal winners Petra Majdic, a cross-country skier from Slovenia, and Joannie Rochette, a Canadian figure skater. "Watching Petra and Joannie, and their determination to carry on and triumph," said Betty Fox, "is something Canadians and the world will not forget. They represent the best of us and what we can accomplish — just like Terry."

The opening ceremony of the 2010 Winter Paralympics included a stirring film tribute to Terry. At the end of the film, Rolly and Betty Fox carried in the Paralympic flame.

Over the years, several books have been written and films made about this special young man. NBA star Steve Nash directed a TV documentary about Terry called *Into the Wind*. In the TV movie *Terry*, through actor Shawn Ashmore, millions of people relived Terry's journey on his Marathon of Hope, as he struggled, overcame the pain and struggled again. They were left with a final image of him running down a lonely road. Then he simply disappears.

But his cause has not. When Terry's run was over, he said, "Even if I don't finish, we need others to continue. It's got to keep going without me." So perhaps the greatest honour given to Terry Fox is that others *have* carried on in his name. With each step taken in the Terry Fox Runs, with each dollar raised through selfless generosity, the world is a little closer to finding cures for the cancers that continue to cause so much suffering. Although Terry said that he was not a dreamer, he believed firmly in the power of miracles. So do all the people who carry on his Marathon of Hope.

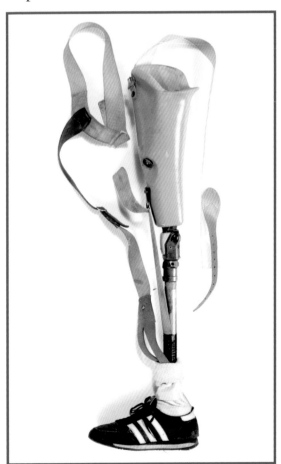

You can find out more about the Terry Fox Run and the Terry Fox Foundation at www.terryfoxrun.org, or call toll free 1-888-836-9786. Marathon of Hope memorabilia can be seen at the Terry Fox Library in Port Coquitlam and at the B.C. Sports Hall of Fame (Terry Fox Gallery) in Vancouver.

There are also several books about Terry:
Terry, by Douglas Coupland: a pictorial work with text for adults
Terry Fox: His Story, by Leslie Scrivener: a biography for adults
Run, by Eric Walters: a young adult novel

My thanks to the Fox family for their generous input, and to my agent, Lynn Bennett, for her support. Thanks as well to Andrea Casault, Diane Kerner, Heather Patterson, Solange Champagne-Cowle, Brigitte Surreau, and a small army of Scholastic staffers who made this book come together.
— *Maxine Trottier*